52773969R00121

Made in the USA
Columbia, SC
06 March 2019